YOUR LAND
AND
MY LAND
The Middle
East

We Visit

KUWAIT

Kathleen

Tracy

Mitchell Lane
PUBLISHERS
P.O. Box 196
Hockessin, Delaware 19707

YOUR LAND
AND
MY LAND
The Middle East

Afghanistan
Iran
Iraq
Israel
Kuwait
Oman
Pakistan
Saudi Arabia
Turkey
Yemen

YOUR LAND AND MY LAND
The Middle East

We Visit KUWAIT

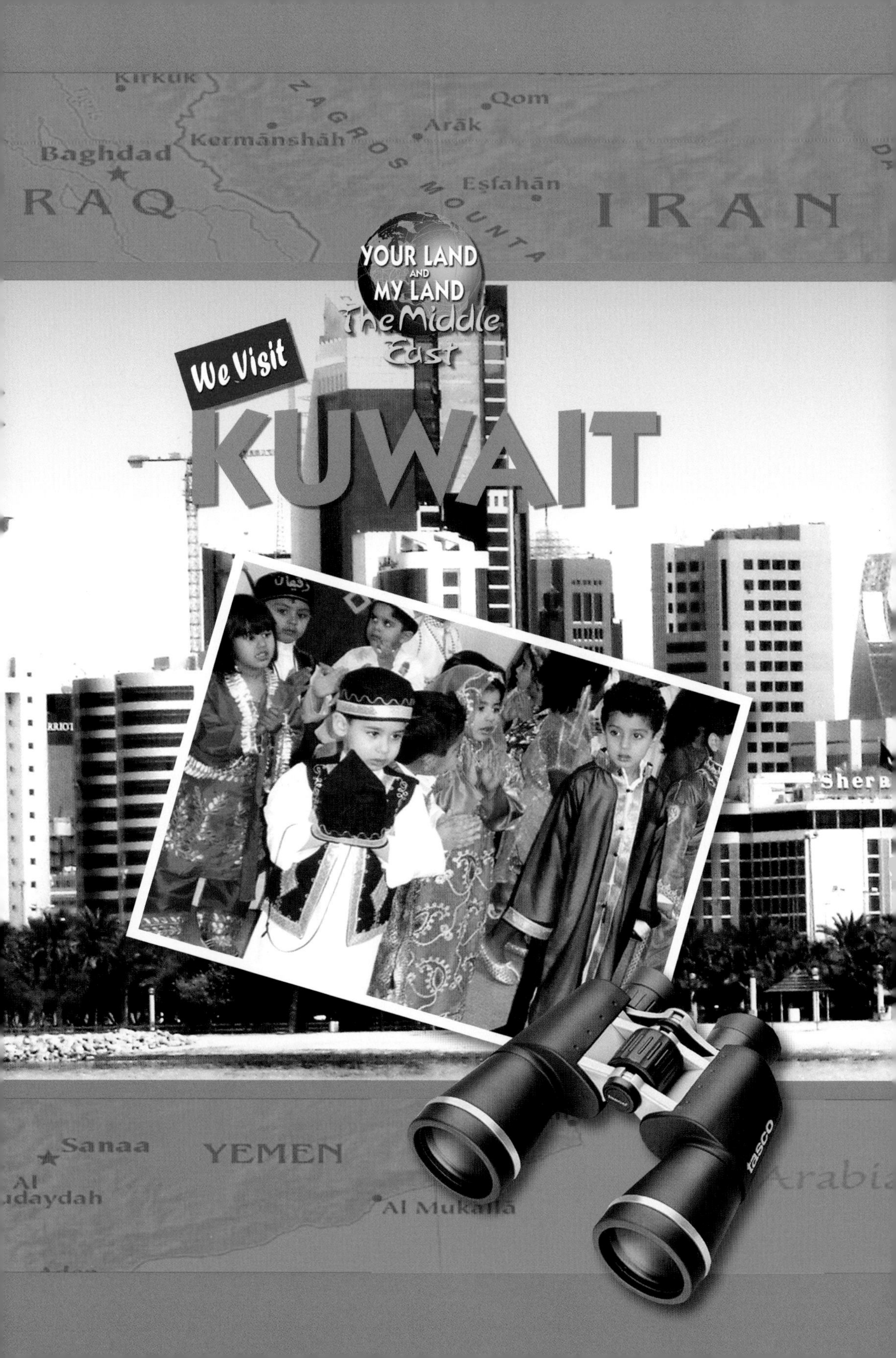

Mitchell Lane
PUBLISHERS

Printing   1   2   3   4   5   6   7   8   9

Library of Congress Cataloging-in-Publication Data
Tracy, Kathleen.
We visit Kuwait / by Kathleen Tracy.
      p. cm. — (Your land and my land: the Middle East)
Includes bibliographical references and index.
ISBN 978-1-58415-958-2 (library bound)
1. Kuwait—Juvenile literature. I. Title.
DS247.K8T73 2011
953.67—dc22
                                                            2011002756

eBook ISBN: 9781612281001

PUBLISHER'S NOTE: This story is based on the author's extensive research, which she believes to be accurate. Documentation of this research is on page 60.

The Internet sites referenced herein were active as of the publication date. Due to the fleeting nature of some web sites, we cannot guarantee they will all be active when you are reading this book.

PLB

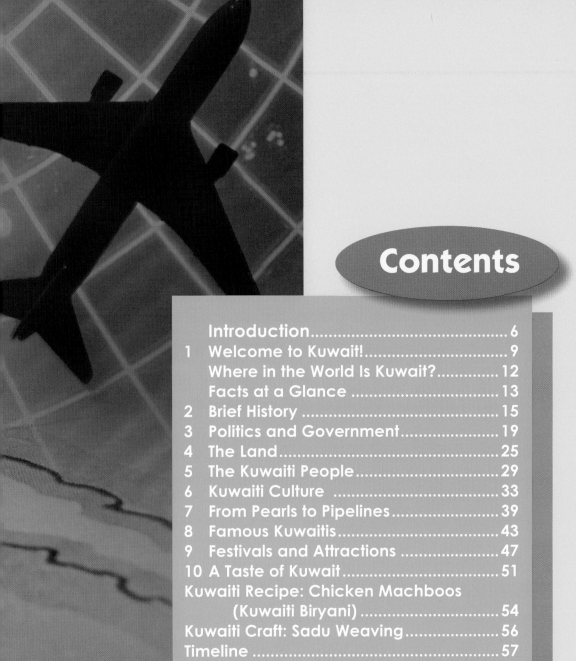

Contents

Introduction

It is the most ancient of lands and home to the three most followed religions on earth. It is the birthplace of human civilization and a region torn by near continual tribal war. It is the inspiration for magical legends and the site of archaeological treasures. It is a devout realm of mosques supported by fields of oil wells. Complex, enigmatic, and compelling, the Middle East is one of the most intriguing, and misunderstood, areas in the world.

The term *Middle East* is relatively new. For centuries, Europeans referred to the region as the Near East. The earliest reference to "Middle East" occurred in a 1902 article published in the British journal, *National Review*; so-called because it was midway between Britain and India.[1] Later, it was popularized by *London Times* journalist Valentine Chirol who was based in Tehran.[2] The residents initially resisted the term but now accept it as a modern geographical point of reference.

However, there is ongoing debate over which countries comprise the Middle East. Some say Armenia, Azerbaijan, and even Pakistan should be included, mostly because they are predominantly Islamic

countries. The more conservative consensus is that the Middle East is the area bordered by Egypt to the west, the Arab Peninsula to the south, and Iran to the east.

Although the Middle Eastern countries share a common language and, most important, a common dominant religion, there are significant differences between the countries, with each having a distinct culture and history. In this book we'll explore Kuwait, one of the most socially tolerant Islamic countries in the world.

The countries of the Middle East include Bahrain, Cyprus, Egypt, Iran, Iraq, Israel, Jordan, Kuwait, Lebanon, Oman, Qatar, Saudi Arabia, Syria, Turkey, United Arab Emirates, and Yemen. The Gaza Strip and the West Bank, which are Palestinian territories, are also part of the Middle East.

It should be noted that while all countries in the Middle East, except Israel, are considered Muslim countries, not all Muslim countries are in the Middle East.

 Al-Safat Square in Kuwait City stands where the old Al-Safat Yard, or marketplace, used to be. In the early days of Kuwait, Al-Safat Yard was a meeting place for traders to come and sell their wares, attracting large numbers of people from the surrounding areas. The old yard was renovated in 1988, and a monument with a single sail in the center was built.

Welcome to Kuwait!

It is one of the smallest Arabic countries but one of the wealthiest per capita. Its capital city is a modern, glistening, sophisticated metropolis but the rest of the country is mostly deserted, undeveloped, and much the same as it has been for thousands of years. Relatively speaking, it's one of the most democratic Islamic countries, even though it has been ruled by the same royal family for two centuries. Kuwait's economic strength—oil—is also its Achilles heel: unless the country develops additional industries, it could revert to a poverty-stricken land of nomadic tribes once its oil reserves are gone.

Over the course of its history, however, Kuwait has proven to be resilient, partly because of its location. Nestled between Iraq and Saudi Arabia along the Persian Gulf, the area has been an important trade hub since the time of Alexander the Great. When Alexander's army passed through the Middle East on its way to India, the invaders colonized one of Kuwait's islands in the Persian Gulf and named it Ikaros. Now known as Failaka (or Faylakah), the island became a bustling trading post between 300 and 100 BCE.[1] Pearls and incense were among the more popular items.

Kuwait, which is approximately the size of New Jersey, is situated at the northwest corner of the Persian Gulf. Its fortuitous location made it the gateway to its region of the Middle East. Because its port welcomed traders and visitors from Africa, Europe, and Eastern Asia, the locals became tolerant and accepting of people from a wide variety

of backgrounds, religions, and ethnic heritages. Kuwait became a melting pot that took advantage of its diversity to prosper and grow.

Unlike many African and Middle Eastern countries, Kuwait has never been a colony. The Kuwaiti people have a long tradition of self-rule, enabling the country to develop cultural characteristics unique to its people. Socially, Kuwaitis are very clan- and tribe-oriented with a deep loyalty to family. However, they are not insular. After the discovery of oil led to wider-ranging prosperity, the Kuwaitis used their wealth to promote the arts as well as political and social awareness. While their history and traditions are revered, Kuwait is also a modern country that manages to balance respect for the past with appreciation for progress.

Like the rest of the Arabian Peninsula, Kuwait is significantly defined by its climate and geography. From April to September it is scorching hot, and less than one half percent of the country is forested.[2] Whereas Saudi Arabia has spectacular and dramatic sand deserts, Kuwait's landscape is mainly a flat, low-lying, often gravelly barren desert. As a result, most of the population lives along the more temperate coast in Kuwait City.

Kuwait City

You may be surprised to learn that even though Kuwait is one of the smallest countries in the world, it is the eighth wealthiest nation per capita on earth.[3] Nearly 90 percent of its revenues come from exporting oil, which was first discovered in the 1930s. Kuwait possesses a fifth of the world's oil supply, and from the end of World War II until 2008, it was the world's second-largest oil exporter. It is still the fifth-largest exporter of oil in the world.[4] Half of the country's revenue goes to the ruling sheikh, who spends most of his wealth on the education and welfare of the Kuwaiti people and the modernization of the kingdom.

The oil industry attracts workers from many other countries seeking employment. There are so many visiting workers that Kuwaitis make up only about half of the entire population; the other half of the population are foreign nationals.[5] The same diversity that made Ikaros a vibrant trading post during the time of Alexander the Great is one of Kuwait's modern strengths, making it a fascinating, and welcoming, multiracial and multicultural country to visit.

Where in the World

IRAQ

IRAN

Ābādān

Khosrowābād

Safwān

'Abdalī

Umm Qaşr

Warbah

Al Fāw

Nahr-e Qaşr

Khawr 'Abd Allāh

Ar Rawḑatayn

Būbiyān

agreed-upon maritime boundary

AL JAHRAH

Jal Az-Zor

Qaşr as Sabīyah

Maskān

Kuwait Bay

Az Zawr

Faylakah

P e r s i a

Wādī al Bāṭin

Al Abraq

Al Jahrah

Ad Dāwhah (Doha)

Kuwait

As Salimīyah

AL KU...

'Awhah

G u l f

Al Farwānīyah

Hawalli

WALLĪ

AL FARWĀNĪYAH

Salemy

Al Maqwā'

Al Aḩmadī

Al Fuhayhil

Mīnā' al Aḩmadī

Ash Shu'aybah

Mīnā' 'Abd Allāh

Kubbar

AL AḨMADĪ

Qārūh

Mīnā' Su'ūd

Al Khiran

'Umm al Marādim

Al Wafrah

Qaşr

Ra's al Khafjī

SAUDI ARABIA

Kuwait

——— International boundary
— · — Governorate *(muḩāfaẓah)* boundary
★ National capital
◉ Governorate *(muḩāfaẓah)* capital
+—+—+ Railroad   ▢ Built-up area
═══ Expressway
——— Road

Governorate boundaries are approximate.

0   10   20   30 Kilometers
0   10   20   30 Miles
Lambert Conformal Conic Projection, SP 12N/38N

Kuwait is situated at the northwest corner of the Persian Gulf. It is bordered by Iran to the northeast, Iraq to the northwest, and Saudi Arabia to the west and south.

KUWAIT FACTS AT A GLANCE

Official Country Name: State of Kuwait

Language: Arabic, although English is widely spoken

Population: 2,789,000 (July 2010 est.)

Area: 6,880 square miles (17,818 square kilometers), about the size of New Jersey

Climate: average 75°F (24°C); highest average 113°F (45°C) in July; 46°F (8°C) in January

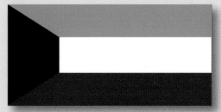

Arfaj

Capital City: Kuwait City

Government: Constitutional emirate

Ethnic makeup: Kuwaiti (45 percent), other Arab (35 percent), South Asian (9 percent), Iranian (4 percent)

Religion: Muslim—85 percent (Sunni 70 percent, Shia 30 percent), other (includes Christian, Hindu, Parsi)

Climate: dry desert; intensely hot summers; short, cool winters

Average rainfall: 3.8 inches (10 centimeters) per year

Lowest point: sea level at Persian Gulf

Highest point: officially Ash-Shaqaya at 951 feet (290 meters), although an unnamed peak reaches 1,003 feet (306 meters)

Longest River: Kuwait has no rivers

National flower: Arfaj (*Rhanterum epapposum*)

Flag: Kuwait's flag was adopted on September 7, 1961. The colors are symbolic: black stands for defeating enemies; white represents purity; green denotes fertile fields; and red depicts blood on Kuwaiti swords. The flag's color scheme was inspired by a poem by Safie Al-Deen Al-Hali:

> White for our work
> Black for our struggles
> Green for our spring homes
> Red for our past

When hanging the flag horizontally, the green stripe should be on top; when hanging vertically, the green stripe should be on the right.

Sources: CIA *World Factbook*, Kuwait, https://www.cia.gov/library/publications/the-world-factbook/geos/ku.html, Embassy of the State of Kuwait, http://www.kuwaitembassy.se/index.php?option=com_content&view=article&id=49&Itemid=56, U.S. Department of State, Kuwait, http://www.state.gov/r/pa/ei/bgn/35876.htm

Located in the Persian Gulf off the coast of Kuwait, Failaka Island is the site of an ancient Greek settlement established by Alexander the Great in the fouth century BCE. The island was also home to the Dilmuns, one of the oldest civilizations in the Middle East.

Brief History

The piece of desert that is today Kuwait was first inhabited 10,000 years ago by nomadic Stone Age peoples. The oldest known permanent settlement, located on the northern shore of Kuwait Bay, dates back to 4500 BCE.[1]

Archaeologists have excavated pottery fragments, beads, and knives known to be used by the Ubaidians, who originated in the Fertile Crescent between the Tigris and Euphrates rivers, in what is now modern Iraq. The Ubaidians were farmers and fishermen but they are best known for their terra-cotta pottery. The Ubaidians were responsible for inventing the tournette, which made their pottery easier to manufacture and paint.[2]

The Ubaidians of Mesopotamia were eventually assimilated into the Sumerian culture; those that ended up in the southern Arabian Peninsula were influenced by the Dilmun civilization, which reached its peak between 2300 and 1000 BCE.[3]

The Dilmuns were Bahrain's earliest recorded settlers, and they eventually dominated their surrounding area as successful maritime traders. They established a settlement on the island known as Failaka, which the Greeks would later name Ikaros. When the Indus Valley civilizations in western India began to decline, the Dilmuns' ability to trade was undercut, and their culture was eventually assimilated into the Babylonian Empire. By the time Alexander the Great arrived, around 326 BCE, Failaka was once again a sleepy island with little evidence the Dilmuns had ever been there.[4]

Failaka was renamed Ikaros, after the Greek mythological character Icarus. His father, Daedalus, created wings so that they could fly. When Icarus got too close to the sun, the wax holding the feathers on his wings melted, and Daedalus watched his son plummet to his death. Some stories say Alexander named it after a similar-looking Greek island where Icarus was believed to be buried. Other versions claim it got its name because it was so hot, it felt as if it were as close to the sun as Icarus had flown.[5]

Alexander established a trading post on Ikaros, and the island was briefly once again a busy port. But when Alexander's empire broke up, Failaka's settlement was abandoned. For the next millennium, the island and its adjacent mainland area were aligned with a succession of states and kingdoms that would come to power for a short time then fade. At the end of the fifteenth century, the Banu Khalid tribe occupied the area from modern Basra to Qatar. The Banu Khalid resisted the Ottoman Turks and effectively ran them out of the area by 1670 CE. Soon after, wealthy Arab families began to settle in the area, drawn by the lush coastal region.[6]

Originally, Kuwait was named al-Qurain. The name Kuwait, which comes from the Arabic word for fort (*kout*) came about after the sheikh Barrak Al Sabah built a fort in al-Qurain and used it as a summer house.[7]

In the early 1700s, several families belonging to the Al Aniza tribe migrated from famine-stricken central Arabia to the northern shore of the Gulf and settled in Kuwait, still a small village. The house of Khalid fell from power and the Al Sabah tribe assumed power. They were named official rulers of Kuwait in 1752. The new rulers established a thriving port economy fueled by fishing, trade, and pearls, then Kuwait's only natural resource.[8]

Because of its small size, Kuwait remained potentially vulnerable to its powerful neighbors, which included Saudi Arabia and land controlled by the Ottoman Turks. To ensure its independence, specifically from the Ottomans, Sheikh Mubarak Al Sabah, often called

Mubarak the Great, entered into an alliance with Great Britain in 1899. Kuwait remained independent but would be politically assisted and militarily defended by Great Britain. When Mubarak died in 1915, Kuwait's population was just 35,000, the majority of whom lived in the city; the rest of the country was largely uninhabited and without definitive borders.

It wasn't until the twentieth century that Kuwait finally established official borders with Iraq to the north and Saudi Arabia to the south, made all the more important by the discovery of oil and the development of the country's petroleum industry in the 1930s. Oil continues to form the basis of Kuwait's wealth.[9]

Kuwait became fully independent from Great Britain in 1961. Under the leadership of Sheikh Sabah al-Salim Al Sabah in the 1960s and '70s, Kuwait established itself as a modern, diverse country that embraces both its traditional past and a technology-driven future.

FYI FACT:

In ancient times the island of Bahrain was known for its breathtaking beauty. The Sumerian poem *Epic of Gilgamesh*, considered one of the first works of ancient literature, refers to Bahrain as the paradise of Dilmun, leading some scholars to believe it was the location of the original Garden of Eden.[10]

Gilgamesh

Born in 1929, Sheikh Sabah IV (Al-Ahmad Al-Jaber Al-Sabah) assumed leadership of Kuwait on January 29, 2006. Sabah IV has been a progressive leader, ushering through laws strengthening freedom of the press, and advocating for women's rights.

Politics and Government

In movies and books, Arab sheikhs are often portrayed as living in opulent palaces surrounded by attendants who cater to their every whim. In the case of oil-rich Kuwait, that characterization isn't too far from the truth. But the early rulers lived more modestly.

The Sabah family has ruled Kuwait since 1752 when Sheikh Sabah I Bin Jaber was named the leader by the other Arabs who had settled near the Bay of Kuwait. Even since then, Kuwait has been ruled by a Sabah. Until Mubarak al Sabah—Mubarak the Great—leadership was often decided by one brother overthrowing or killing another to assume power. Now it is chosen by family council.[1]

Mubarak himself overthrew his brother to become emir in 1896. But he successfully established a peaceful process of succession, and after his death in 1915, his two eldest sons were the next in line. Jaber II ruled until 1917, followed by Salim, who died in 1921. The next ruler was sheikh Jaber's son, Ahmad, who led Kuwait for 29 years, until 1950. Next came Abdallah al-Salim, a descendent of sheikh Salim and the ruler many Kuwaitis consider the father of their country for guiding the nation into its "Oil Age."[2]

The emir, or leader, appoints members to his cabinet and names a prime minister. Traditionally, the prime minister's post was given to the crown prince. Beginning in 2003, the two positions were officially separated, and a different family member is now appointed Kuwait's prime minister. Traditionally, the Sabah family has also appointed relatives to the key cabinet positions, such as the foreign, defense, interior,

Kuwait's Emirs

1. Sheikh Sabah I Bin Jaber: 1752–1762
2. Sheikh Abdullah I: 1762–1814
3. Sheikh Jaber I: 1814–1859
4. Sheikh Sabah II: 1859–1866
5. Sheikh Abdullah II: 1866–1892
6. Sheikh Mohammad I: 1892–1896
7. Sheikh Mubarak Al-Sabah: 1896–1915
8. Sheikh Jaber II: 1915–1917
9. Sheikh Salim Al-Mubarak: 1917–1921
10. Sheikh Ahmad Al-Jaber Al Sabah: 1921–1950
11. Sheikh Abdallah III Al-Salim Al-Sabah: 1950–1965
12. Sheikh Sabah Al-Salim Al Sabah: 1965–1977
13. Sheikh Jaber III Al-Ahmad Al-Jaber Al Sabah: 1977–2006
14. Sheik Sabah IV Al-Ahmad Al-Jaber Al Sabah: 2006–

and finance ministers. The emir has sole executive power as well as veto power, but there is also a national assembly, the Majlis al-Umma. It has 50 elected Majlis who consult and help prepare legislation. The Majlis serve four-year terms.[3]

Kuwait does not have any formal political parties. While there are obviously no executive elections, people can vote for the legislature. Police officers and members of the military are not allowed to vote.

Kuwait is among the most progressive Arabic Middle Eastern countries when it comes to women's rights. In 2009, the first group of female police cadets graduated. The ceremony was attended by Emir Al-Sabah and other dignitaries.

Voting age is 21, and until 2005, only men were allowed to cast a ballot. Starting in 2006, women were allowed to vote and run for office. In July 2005, the first female minister, Massouma al-Mubarak, was appointed planning minister and minister of state for administrative development affairs.[4]

Kuwait is divided into six provinces or governorates. The province of al-Kuwayt includes Kuwait City and the islands off the coast. Hawalli is a heavily populated suburb of Kuwait City and a prosperous commercial center. Al Ahmadi is home to many oil wells. Al Jahra, the largest governorate, is the country's agricultural area. Farwaniyah is where the Kuwait International Airport is located. Mubarak al Kabir governorate was established when Hawalli was split in two.

After Kuwait secured independence from Great Britain, the Iraqi government claimed Kuwait as rightfully part of Iraq—even though Iraq had formally accepted Kuwait's borders on two previous occasions. In 1990, Iraq invaded Kuwait, laying military claim to the country. The emir fled to Saudi Arabia, and Kuwait was under Iraqi rule. In what became known as Operation Desert Storm, armed forces led by the United States defeated Iraq. After six months of Iraqi rule, Kuwait

In 1990, Iraq leader Saddam Hussein invaded Kuwait. A United States–led coalition eventually liberated Kuwait from Iraqi occupation. As they retreated, Iraqi forces set fire to an estimated 700 Kuwaiti oil wells.

was liberated. Although Iraq formally accepted the UN-designated borders, tensions remained between the countries over the borders.[5]

As the Iraqi troops left the country, they set fire to the oil wells, and Kuwait's oil industry had to be rebuilt. The setback was temporary, and within a few years production returned to prewar levels. In 2003, Kuwait allowed U.S.-led forces to stage their operations in the country prior to the invasion of Iraq to oust Saddam Hussein from power.

Although it is a Muslim country, in recent years Kuwait has been the target of attacks by Islamist militants, including some who are believed to have links with Al-Qaeda. Kuwaiti authorities say extremist groups have plotted attacks on Western targets.[6]

Using oil revenues, the Kuwaiti government sponsors many social welfare policies such as retirement income, marriage bonuses, housing loans, free medical services, education, and essentially guaranteed employment. When there is a budget surplus, the emir gives each Kuwaiti citizen who applies for it a cash bonus. None of these services, however, are extended to foreign nationals. Similarly, only citizens can own real estate, banks, or stock in publicly traded companies.

Kuwait and the United States have historically enjoyed good relations. In 2011, the United States was Kuwait's largest supplier of goods and services. Kuwait has also assisted U.S. efforts to stop international terrorism.

Kuwait is known for spectacular sandstorms, which occur when strong dry winds blow over the desert, carrying along clouds of dust that can reduce visibility to near zero. In April 2011, a massive sandstorm covered Saudi Arabia, Iraq, and Kuwait, shutting down air traffic and oil exports from Kuwait.

The Land

Most of mainland Kuwait is a flat desert that slopes slightly to its highest point, an unnamed hill in western Kuwait that is 1,003 feet (306 meters) high. Another peak, Ash-Shaqaya, near Kuwait City in the east, is nearly as tall at 951 feet (290 meters). The country has no mountains, lakes, or rivers but enjoys a coastline that stretches for 310 miles (400 kilometers) along the Persian Gulf. Kuwait Bay forms a natural harbor, and Kuwait City is located along its southern shore. Not all of Kuwait's coastline is postcard perfect. While the area along the Persian Gulf boasts sandy, tourist-friendly beaches, the area around Kuwait Bay is known for mudflats.

Summertime temperatures regularly exceed 110°F (43°C) and dust storms are common. During the short winter season, it can get down into the 50s (teens in Celsius), especially in January, the coldest month. The annual rainfall averages only about 4 inches (10 centimeters) and mostly occurs during the winter. Other than a few aquifers, Kuwait has no natural freshwater sources. It depends on desalination plants that remove the salt from seawater to provide drinking water.[1]

There are nine islands off the coast of Kuwait: Bubiyan, Failaka, Warba, Miskan, Umm Al-Nami, Auhha, Kubbar, Qaruh, and Umm Al-Maradim. There used to be a tenth island, Al-Akkaz, also known as Shuwaikh Island. Located just a half mile off the coast, the island is now a peninsula—it is attached to an industrial area of the mainland via a land bridge.

The largest of the islands is Bubiyan, which is connected to the mainland by a concrete bridge. Flat with little vegetation, Bubiyan doesn't attract many visitors. Most of the islands are uninhabited but have coral reefs and are breeding grounds for turtles and many species of birds, including falcons.[2]

Failaka is considered the most beautiful of the Kuwaiti islands. Before the Gulf War, an estimated 5,000 people lived on Failaka but most were relocated to the mainland during the conflict. Kuwait plans to make Failaka a tourist resort.

Mainland Kuwait is technically considered a semidesert. Despite the blazing heat during summer, its cooler, rainy winters allow for a variety of plant life, including salt marsh plants, desert grass, sand dune shrubs, and annual grass. Areas that get rain during the winter can

Camels are uniquely adapted for desert living, able to go long stretches without drinking water. In addition to being a mode of transportation, camels are also used for entertainment: camel racing is a popular pastime, with races held every Saturday between November and May.

produce flowering plants. In 1983, Kuwait named the Arfaj (*Rhanterum epapposum*) its national flower. Abundant in the central and northeastern part of the desert, it blooms yellow in the spring and is a source of water for camels, which snack on the plant.

Kuwait is home to many species of butterflies, nearly 40 types of reptiles, 280 species of birds (the majority of which are migratory), and a variety of mammals such as hedgehogs, wolves, gazelles, and camels.[3] The grazing style of camels—to eat only part of each plant—actually stimulates plant growth. To protect the plant life from overgrazing by goat and sheep herds kept by Bedouins, the Kuwaiti government has banned grazing in nearly half the country.

One of the most common reptiles is the dinosaur-looking spiny-tailed lizard, or dhub. When threatened, the lizard stands and hisses. Bedouins would catch dhubs and cook them. Less common but equally prehistoric in appearance is the desert monitor, which can grow to 5 feet (1.5 meters) long.

Common snakes include the sand boa, rat snake, and leaf-nosed snake. Kuwait is also home to some poisonous snakes, the most dangerous being the black desert cobra, whose bite can be lethal to humans. According to Bedouin folklore, if a black cobra is killed, its spirit will return to destroy its attacker.

> **FYI FACT:**
>
> The Persian Gulf is the traditional name found on most historic maps, and it is also the name the United Nations uses in its official documents. The Arab League calls it the Arabian Gulf, which is also what the United Nations uses in its Arabic documents.

Spiny-tailed lizard

Black desert cobra

While all Muslim nations observe Ramadan, in Kuwait there is a tradition known as Gurgian which occurs midway through Ramadan where children dress up in colorful costumes and go door to door asking for candy.

The Kuwaiti People

Like the rest of the countries on the Arabian Peninsula, Kuwait is a Muslim country. Globally, an estimated 85 percent of Muslims belong to the Sunni sect; the rest are Shia Muslims. In the Persian Gulf region of the Middle East, the majority of Muslims are Shiites. They form the majority in Iraq and Iran; and although they are minorities in Saudi Arabia, Lebanon, Pakistan, India, Syria and Kuwait, their numbers are still significant.[1]

The Shia and Sunni share the same basic beliefs of Islam, just as Baptists and Catholics both believe Jesus was the son of God. But early in the history of Islam, there was a split caused by a disagreement over leadership. After the death of Muhammad, the founder of Islam, there was a power struggle over who should take his place as the Muslim leader, or caliph. A majority of prominent Muslims believed Muhammad had not named an official successor, and they chose his closest adviser and companion, Abu Bakr, to succeed him. This upset other Muslims who believed Muhammad had chosen his relative, Ali ibn Abi Talib, as his successor.[2]

After Muhammad's death, some of his followers started drifting away from the faith so influential Muslims believed a strong leader was needed to keep the faithful united. Ali did not actively oppose the election of Abu Bakr, but his supporters believed that direct descendants of Muhammad were the only rightful Muslim leaders. They became known as the Shia, a name that came from Shi'at Ali, or "the party of Ali." Those who believed that Islamic leaders should be chosen based on their ability to be both a secular and religious leader became known as the Sunnis. Ali eventually became the fourth caliph, but his brief reign ended with his assassination. The rift between the two sects continues to this day.[3]

Shiites believe that imams—religious leaders who are descendants of Muhammad—have the exclusive right to interpret Islamic law. Sunni Muslims argue that leadership is not a birthright, but needs to be earned and can be given or taken away by the Muslim people.

In Kuwait, 85 percent of the population is Muslim, with 70 percent Sunni and 30 percent Shia. Fifteen percent of the population is non-Muslim including Christian, Hindu, and Parsi.[4]

In 1915, the population of Kuwait was just 35,000. The discovery of oil in 1938 prompted a dramatic influx of foreign nationals, mostly Arabs, seeking work. In 1940, the population had grown to 50,000, and by 1957 it had swelled to over 200,000 people.[5]

Even though the population has increased, the majority of the country remains effectively uninhabited. Over 90 percent of the population still lives within a 300-square-mile (777-square-kilometer) area around Kuwait City and its harbor. Although the majority of the populace is Arab, less than half are from the Arabian Peninsula. After the defeat of Iraq in 1991, the Kuwaiti government limited the entry of foreign nationals from countries that had supported Iraq during the Gulf War. The policy was mostly an effort to reduce the expatriate population. However, the immigration limits were eventually lifted and foreign nationals now make up about half of Kuwait's population.[6]

FYI FACT:

For special occasions in Kuwait, guests may be served traditional Bedouin dishes such as camel meat or whole stuffed lambs.

Al Seif Palace is the reigning monarch's headquarters and government office. The palace's best known feature is the watch tower, which is covered in blue tiles and has a gold-plated dome.

The emir and his family live surrounded by creature comforts, but they also spread the wealth. Kuwait invests heavily in state-funded education and higher education. Since 1965, children between the ages of six and fourteen are required to go to school, though there is free kindergarten beginning at age four, and students usually attend for twelve years after kindergarten. They can choose from government-run schools or private schools, which may also receive funds from the government. Food, books, clothing, and transportation are all free. There are also specialty schools for children of expatriates, who are not allowed to attend the government-run schools. The country's 93 percent literacy rate is one of the highest in the Arab world.

Also, the government pays for qualified students to attend college abroad to earn degrees not offered at Kuwait University. In 2009, over 3,000 Kuwaiti students attended American colleges and universities.[7]

While religion may be the most obvious bond among Kuwaitis, it is only one aspect of their culture, which is a rich tapestry of modern sensibilities interwoven with reverence for their nomadic traditions.

Kuwait has a long history of enjoying live theater. There are several theaters operating throughout the year, including the popular Kuwait Little Theatre that puts on approximately six productions each year.

Kuwaiti Culture

When Americans think of "nightlife," they usually imagine nightclubs, music venues, and bars. In Kuwait, nightlife is just as social but more sober—literally. Since alcohol is prohibited in Kuwait, there are no Western-type bars or nightclubs. Instead, Kuwaitis spend their evenings out walking along the main streets, shopping in the old-style souks and modern malls, and enjoying leisurely dinners at restaurants or late-evening weather at outdoor coffee shops. There are Starbucks coffee shops in Kuwait, but for a cup of traditional java, people gather at coffee shops known as *maqahas*.

Movies are a favored pastime, as are live poetry recitals. For tourists, some of the major hotels sometimes feature live music. Kuwait also has a long tradition of live theater, which was first performed in Kuwait City in the early 1920s. In 1952, the Kuwait Players was established. The troupe, which performs in English, stages many productions each year, from Shakespeare to children's shows.[1]

Shopping is a full-time pursuit for many Kuwaitis, and the city is home to many malls, such as the exclusive Salhiya Mall, the Souk Sharq Mall in downtown, and the Villa Moda, which is full of designer stores. Shoppers can buy Persian rugs, spices, high fashion, or traditional clothing.

Kuwaiti women are known for being very fashion-minded. They dress in the latest Western styles, although modesty is followed. For certain festivals, traditional clothing may be worn, such as the *thob*, a

In keeping with the Islamic tradition of modesty, most Muslim women wear a *hijab*, or headscarf. However, there are those who interpret the Koran's call for modesty less strictly and opt against wearing a head covering.

long overdress used when dancing. When out shopping or dining in public, many women wear a silk cloak called an *aba* over their clothes.

Since many people who live in Kuwait are foreign nationals who come from more conservative countries, it is common to see some women wearing burqas, veils that cover the entire face except for the eyes. A scarf called the *hijab* is also worn by many non-Kuwaiti Muslim women. It covers the head and hair but leaves the face visible.

Food is important in Kuwaiti culture, especially during festivals. Seafood, rice, and meats——such as beef, chicken, and lamb—are staples. Dishes are often made with lots of spices such as cinnamon, cloves, nutmeg, pepper, and paprika. Traditional meals include roasted lamb stuffed with rice, hummus, stuffed vine leaves, and meat kebabs. Desserts tend to be very sweet, such as dates or baklava. Since alcohol is forbidden, coffee and tea are usually consumed, along with sweet, drinkable yogurt.[2]

FYI FACT:

Consuming or possessing pork is illegal in Kuwait, and the meat may be confiscated upon arrival.

Tabeekh is a traditional Kuwaiti cooking method. All the food to be served is put into a single container, then cooked together. Another local cooking style is called *marag*, where all the main ingredients are prepared by frying them separately, then added all together and cooked over low heat.[3]

In Kuwaiti families, men and women eat together, unless unrelated males are present. At parties, men and women tend to be segregated. Either way, meals are a time to relax and converse. Large dinners with extended family are regular occurrences. Kuwaitis are known for their hospitality, and guests are always welcome. They are also expected to take seconds to show they are happy with the food. So if you're ever in a Kuwaiti home, wear loose pants!

Despite the sophistication of its cities, national identity is still rooted in tradition. It is impossible to separate Kuwaiti culture from the country's Islamic heritage. Many of the national festivals are religion-based. Daily prayer is a part of life. Mosques are filled every day with the faithful.

Sometimes the old ways blend with the new in interesting ways. For example, many city dwellers enjoy camping trips as a way to connect with the country's Bedouin heritage. However, unlike the famous desert nomads who crossed the desert with little more than their clothes and simple tents, modern Kuwaiti campers pitch sturdy canvas tents, use generators that provide electricity, and stay in contact with work and home via their cell phones, charged by power adapters in their vehicles.

Another Bedouin tradition is falconry. Many Kuwaitis breed falcons and keep them for hunting or simply as homage to the tradition. Falcons are considered intelligent and can be trained. Falconers say the birds form a bond with their owners within a matter of weeks. In 2007, there was a scare about bird flu, and thousands of falcons were brought in for testing by their owners. Fortunately only a handful of the birds were diagnosed with the disease.

Falconry is a national pastime in Kuwait. Originally, hunters on horseback used the birds to help them catch game in the desert. Now they hunt from four-wheelers. The Saker and the Peregrine are the most popular falcons, and white falcons are especially prized.

Soccer has become very popular in Kuwait and the country now has a national team that competes internationally. Kuwait's National Stadium, located in the city of Safat, was designed with a membrane roof to shield fans from the torrid desert heat.

As with most cultures, the arts are a reflection of society. For example, Kuwaiti literature is strongly based on ancient Bedouin folklore, again showing the strong affinity of the culture to its past. The native music of the country has a distinct sound, a combination of East African and Indian music that was influenced by traders who passed through Kuwait. A more modern style of Kuwait music is called *sawt*, popularized in the 1970s. Described as bluesy but with techno-pop elements, Kuwaiti *sawt* bands, especially the Al-Budoor Band, are popular throughout the Gulf region.[4]

Kuwait's diverse culture has made it a popular vacation destination both within and outside the Middle East, so tourism is a growing industry. Although currently oil-rich, the Kuwaiti government knows it is important to develop other industries to ensure continued prosperity.

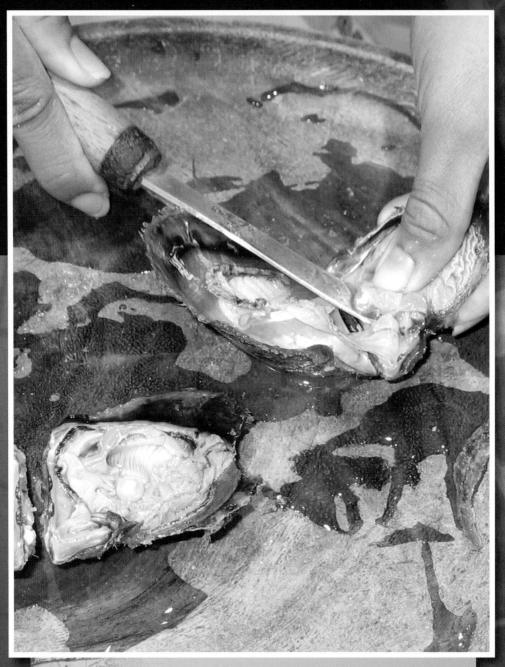

 Pearls are harvested from oysters. Before oil was discovered, pearling was Kuwait's main industry. Today, pearl diving is one of the more popular tourist activities. Pearl diving season peaks in June.

From Pearls to Pipelines

For several centuries, pearls were Kuwait's only natural resource and its primary source of commerce. Every year, as many as 800 ships arrived at the end of summer to cultivate the local pearl banks. As a result, a shipbuilding industry evolved in Kuwait, although the country needed to import the building materials. As previously mentioned, trading was also a mainstay, as caravans traveling between India and the Mediterranean countries stopped in Kuwait to sell their goods. The introduction of Japanese cultured pearls combined with the 1929 stock market crash and resulting worldwide depression effectively ended Kuwait's pearl industry.[1]

Throughout the 1920s and '30s, Kuwait's economy struggled, and the country was one of the poorest in the region. Then on a rainy February 22, 1938, oil was discovered in the Burgan field of Kuwait. There was so much oil that when the well was first tapped, it couldn't be controlled until workers plugged the hole with a 60-foot- (18-meter-) long pole. That first well continues to produce oil.[2]

It would take almost a decade before the first oil shipment was ready. According to the Kuwait Petroleum Corporation:

> At 7 o'clock in the morning of the 30th of June, 1946 a grand celebration was occasioned by exporting the first Kuwait's oil shipment. . . . Mr. Southwell, Director of Kuwait Oil Company Ltd., London, started the event by receiving Sheikh Ahmad Al-Jaber Al-Sabah and his companions and escorting them to

On June 30, 1946, Sheikh Ahmad opened the valve that let Kuwait's crude oil flow through an offshore pipeline to waiting British tankers. Oil remains the country's primary industry.

the ceremony site, where the silver wheel had been placed to herald the occasion. Sheikh Ahmad turned the wheel to start the first Kuwait's crude oil shipment flowing smoothly through an offshore pipeline to the British tanker Fusilier. 10,567 tons of crude oil was loaded in 11 hours and 13 minutes.[3]

Since then, Kuwait has enjoyed continuous prosperity. But the Kuwaiti leaders have sought to develop other industries, such as tourism. Historically, there has been very little agriculture, although desalination plants have allowed for some farming.

According to *Forbes* magazine, in 2009, the Kuwait government "passed an economic development plan that pledges to spend up to $140 billion in five years to diversify the economy away from oil, attract more investment, and boost private sector participation in the economy."[4] The government has invested in paper and cement manufacturing, along with a modest fishing industry. But none of this would have been possible without the revenue brought in by oil.

It is estimated that Kuwait's oil deposits amount to 100 billion barrels, almost a tenth of the total known reserves on earth. Over two million barrels are produced daily. If that rate is maintained, the reserves will last until approximately 2025. Currently, without oil revenue, which accounts for 95 percent of the country's wealth, Kuwait would not have the resources to sustain its population.[5]

The Kuwait Stock Exchange (KSE) was established in 1962. The KSE is one of the first and largest stock exchanges in the Persian Gulf region.

Kuwait's economic health is important to the entire region because through Kuwait's Fund for Arab Economic Development (KFAED), the country has given approximately $15 billion in financial aid to many developing countries all over the world, building goodwill while establishing trading partners of the future.[6]

The Kuwait workweek goes from Saturday to Wednesday, with Thursday and Friday as the national weekend. However, banks and other financial companies work Sundays through Thursdays, so they can more easily do business with international money and trading markets.[7]

Government offices are open 7:30 to 1:30 in the winter and 7:00 to 1:00 in the summer. Private businesses make their own hours, but in general, shops are open from 8:30 to noon, then again from 4:30 to 9:30. During the holy month of Ramadan, business hours are much shorter, because worship takes precedence over commerce.

Zed Al Refai is one of the world's most renowned explorers and mountain climbers. Born in 1966, he is the first Arab to scale the seven highest summits on the seven continents.

Famous Kuwaitis

Although not household names in Western countries, these homegrown heroes are revered within Kuwait for their unique accomplishments.

Zed Al Refai

Zed "Zeddy" Al Refai, born October 28, 1966, is one of the world's most renowned explorers and mountain climbers. Born in Kuwait, Al Refai was educated in Finland as a youth then attended college in the United States, studying in Florida, New Jersey, and Pennsylvania. During school vacations he would trek through the Rockies or other mountain ranges.[1]

Al Refai moved to Switzerland in 1992 and a few years later took a vacation to Nepal, where he became entranced by Mount Everest, which is in the Himalayas. After training for several years climbing smaller peaks, in 1999, Al Refai became the first Arab to summit Denali–Mount McKinley (20,320 feet/6,194 meters), which is the highest peak in North America. He is also the first Arab to scale the seven highest summits on the seven continents, which besides McKinley includes Carstensz Pyramid in Oceania (2000, 16,024 feet/4,884 meters); Elbrus in Europe (2000, 18,442 feet/5,621 meters); Kilimanjaro in Africa (2001, 19,298 feet/5,882 meters); Everest in Asia (2003, 29,029 feet/8,848 meters); Vinson Massif in Antarctica (2004, 16,050 feet/4,892 meters); and Aconcagua in South America (2004, 22,841 feet/6,962 meters). He also scaled the modest Mount Kosciuszko in Australia (2005, 7,310 feet/2,228 meters).[2]

Al Refai is director of the Arabian Mountaineering and Alpine Climbing Club, which he founded to popularize mountain climbing among people in the Middle East.

Ahmad Meshari Al-Adwani[3]

Ahmad Meshari Al-Adwani was a writer, poet, and teacher best known for writing the lyrics to Kuwait's national anthem.

Al-Adwani was born in 1923 in Kuwait's Qibla neighborhood. A year after graduating from secondary school in 1938, he traveled to Cairo and enrolled in the College of Arabic Language Studies at the Al-Azhar University, which was founded in 988 CE and is the second oldest college in Egypt, behind Cairo University.

After graduating, Al-Adwani established the monthly magazine *Al-Be'thah* in Cairo, with his friend and lifelong companion, Dr. Abdulaziz Hussein. He would go on to found several other magazines throughout his life.

Along with Dr. Hussein, Al-Adwani helped found many cultural and social programs in Kuwait that promoted the arts and education. Between 1957 and 1965, he implemented the Teaching of the Arabic Language Curriculum in the Department of Information, in addition to helping prepare the curricula of other school systems in the Persian Gulf area.

Among the programs he championed were the Fine Arts Gallery, the Department of Arabian Culture, and the Department of Musical Culture. In 1973, by decree of the emir, he was appointed as the Director of the National Council for Culture, the Arts, and Letters.

Al-Adwani died in 1990 at the age of 67, leaving behind a trove of unpublished scripts and poems.

FYI FACT:

The first high school for girls in Kuwait was opened in 1959.

Massouma al-Mubarak

Dr. Massouma al-Mubarak was Kuwait's first female cabinet member. She graduated from Kuwait University in 1971 with a degree in political science, then went to the United States to continue her education. She obtained a master's degree in political science from Northern Texas University in 1976 and a second master's in international relations from the University of Denver, along with her PhD. While in the United States, she learned what it was like for a woman to live in a free society.[4]

"When I was in the States, I joined the feminist movement there," she told *ABC News*. "Definitely such participation raises my awareness. Then when I came here [Kuwait], I joined the groups, women activists, and ever since I am working on it."[5]

Once back in Kuwait, al-Mubarak became an advocate for women's issues to raise attention and awareness about women's status, she says. Her writing is credited with helping Kuwaiti women get the right to vote and the right to hold public office in 2005. That same year al-Mubarak was appointed Kuwait's first female cabinet minister, as Minister of Planning and Minister of State for Administrative Development Affairs. She was later named Minister of Health.[6]

In the 2009 elections, al-Mubarak and three other women became the first females to join the Kuwaiti parliament.

Al-Mubarak is aware that many Arabs remain skeptical about women being in politics. "Some are looking or waiting for me to prove to them that I am a capable woman," she told *ABC News*, "but I am telling you that time will prove, my achievement will prove, if I am capable or not."[7]

Massouma al-Mubarak

The twentieth anniversary of Sheikh Sabah IV becoming emir was a national holiday. Part of the festivities included a massive fireworks display by the Kuwait Towers, located on the Arabian Gulf. A main tourist attraction, the towers are covered in 55,000 steel plates painted in eight different colors.

Festivals and Attractions

As in other Arab nations, festivals and holidays in Kuwait celebrate both their religious devotion and their patriotism. But Kuwaitis also enjoy some secular attractions that appeal as much to tourists as they do to locals.

The Eid al Adha, or Feast of Sacrifice, is observed at the end of the annual Hajj, which is the yearly pilgrimage to Mecca. According to Islamic law, Muslims must make the pilgrimage at least once in their life, unless prevented by some physical or financial hardship. It begins on the tenth day of Dul-Hajj, the sacred month of pilgrimage, and in Kuwait can last from two to ten days. Because the Islamic calendar is based on visible lunar cycles, the exact dates of the feast vary.

The month of Ramadan is a time of personal reflection, spiritual renewal, and strict fasting by day, followed by feasting at night. At the end of Ramadan, Muslims observe an exuberant three-day celebration called Eid al-Fitr, the Festival of Fast-Breaking.

Before the start of Eid, each Muslim family gives a donation of food to the poor, such as rice, barley, and dates, to ensure that even Muslims in need can have a holiday meal and participate in the celebration. This charitable donation is known as Sadaqa-ul-Fitr, "charity of fast-breaking."

Eid al-Fitr falls on the first day of Shawwal, the month after Ramadan. In the morning, Muslims gather early in outdoor locations or mosques to perform the Eid prayer, which is a sermon followed by

Liberation Tower is the second tallest structure in Kuwait. Originally, the tower was to be called the Kuwait Telecommunications Tower, but after construction was completed in 1993, it was re-christened Liberation Tower to commemorate Kuwait's being freed from Iraqi occupation.

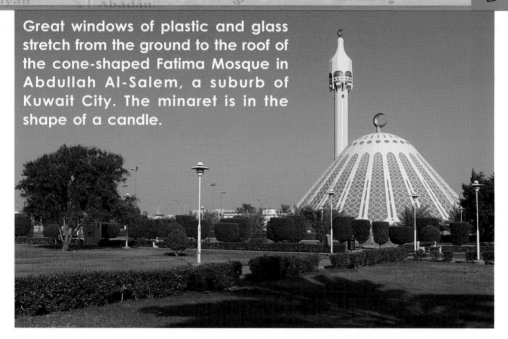

Great windows of plastic and glass stretch from the ground to the roof of the cone-shaped Fatima Mosque in Abdullah Al-Salem, a suburb of Kuwait City. The minaret is in the shape of a candle.

a short congregational prayer. After the prayer is finished, everyone leaves to visit family and friends. It is common to bring gifts, especially to children. The celebration traditionally continues for three days.

Every February 25 Kuwaitis celebrate National Day, which commemorates when Kuwait was founded as a nation in 1961. To show their pride, Kuwaitis wear national dress, participate in public meetings, and get together with family and friends. At night there are fireworks displays, like the ones in the United States on the Fourth of July. Liberation Day is the next day, February 26, and celebrates Kuwait's liberation from Iraq in the Gulf War. This is similar to Memorial Day in the United States.

The Gift Exhibition in Kuwait is a twice-yearly event that is essentially a gift fair that shows off a fun assortment of perfumes, garments, antiques, handicrafts, leather and other items. For the shop-happy Kuwaitis, this is a highly anticipated event.

There are also several trade fairs, including the International Perfumes and Cosmetics Exhibition, the Gold and Jewelry Exhibition, and the Modern House Exhibition. These conferences attract visitors from all over the world. Once in Kuwait, many take time to explore some of the country's other attractions, which range from bird watching and snorkeling to day trips into the desert.

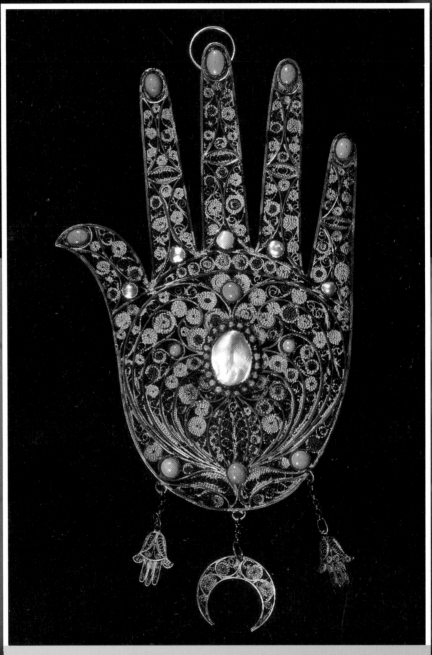

The hamsa is a traditional design in Muslim and Jewish art. The hand, which is often two-thumbed, represents the hand of God (Allah). It is worn as protection against the evil eye; the eye motif on many hamsas represents that power. It is also known as the hand of Fatima, after Fatima Zahra, the Prophet Muhammad's daughter.

Chapter 10

A Taste of Kuwait

Imperial eagle

Kuwait City is the main inhabited area in Kuwait and is where visitors will spend the majority of their time. While Arabic is the official language, many Kuwaitis speak English, so tourists can get by not knowing Arabic, especially in and around Kuwait City. Like most modern cities, there are museums, galleries, and other typical places to visit. But outside the city are many other historical and beautiful sights.

Across Kuwait Bay is the Jal Az-Zor National Park, which is a sanctuary for migratory falcons. These birds, along with black vultures and imperial eagles, gather along the cliffs above the bay. The park spans the Jal Az-Zor ridge and the adjacent coastal area made up of sand dunes, marshes, and mud flats.

Two other popular bird watching areas are also in Kuwait Bay. Dawhat Kazima is a shallow bay that attracts coastal birds such as gray herons, avocets, and migrating waders. The Ad-Doha Nature Reserve is filled with at least 70 species of migratory birds, which are drawn by the reed beds. Sulaibikhat Bay is another area with mud flats that are feeding grounds for wading birds. But the wetlands at the Al-Jahra Pools Nature Reserve provide the best assortment of birds, with over 200 recorded species,

Marsh harrier

such as the buzzard, spotted eagle, steppe eagle, imperial eagle, marsh harrier, lesser kestrel, and black vulture.

For those interested in Kuwait's oil history, the day trip to the Era of Black Gold is highly recommended. The trip includes a visit to the Kuwait Oil Display Museum and visiting the house of a nineteenth-century Kuwaiti merchant. Day trippers can finish off their excursion with a meal of local food offered at nearby Dhow Harbor. Another day trip highlighting the historical significance of Kuwait includes visits to the Kuwait National Museum and Sadu House, the Traditional House of Weaving.

Sadu weaving is a traditional Kuwaiti craft. Visitors can see demonstrations of sadu weaving at the Bayt Sadu (Sadu House) museum.

The waters of the Persian Gulf off the Kuwaiti coast offer some of the best snorkeling in the Middle East.

Visiting Kuwait's islands can be like stepping back into another world. Kubbar is the most popular island during the summer, but Qaruh's coral reef and nesting ground for sea turtles make it a popular destination. The island of Umm Al-Maradim is home to phosphorescent algae that light up the water as if there were fireflies beneath the surface wherever the water is disturbed.

And finally no trip to Kuwait is complete without a visit to the camel market—just make sure to keep your distance, because the camels are known to spit with great accuracy!

Chicken Machboos
(Kuwaiti Biryani)

Get a taste of Kuwait by preparing chicken machboos, a traditional dish also known as Kuwaiti Biryani. You will need **an adult** to help you make this recipe.

Ingredients:
Chicken
1 cinnamon stick
2 cardamom pods
2 or 3 whole cloves
5 black peppercorns
Flour

3 cups basmati rice

Onion-spice topping
2 large yellow onions, finely chopped
1 tablespoon vegetable oil
¼ cup golden raisins, soaked in water
¼ teaspoon ground cardamom
¼ teaspoon dried black lime (*loomi*), or ½ tsp. lime zest
¼ teaspoon ground black pepper
½ teaspoon sugar

Tomato sauce
2 large tomatoes, chopped
2 tablespoons water
2 cloves garlic, crushed
1 tablespoon tomato paste

To Prepare:

1. Rinse chicken inside and out. Place in a pot with enough water to cover the chicken and add cinnamon stick, cardamom pods, cloves, and peppercorns. Bring to a boil, and continue to cook uncovered over medium heat until chicken is done, around 40 minutes. Remove and drain the chicken, saving the broth.

2. Drain the fat off the top of the broth and strain it to remove spices. Prepare three cups of basmati rice according to package directions, using the broth from the chicken instead of water. Add salt to taste.

3. While the rice cooks, brown the onions in a nonstick skillet over medium heat, stirring frequently, until clear. Sprinkle with a little water and stir quickly until onions are brown and the water has evaporated. Stir in oil, drained raisins, spices, and sugar. Cook for one minute. Remove mixture from skillet and set aside.

4. Lightly dust the boiled, drained chicken with flour. In a clean skillet over medium-high heat, brown the chicken, turning frequently, until the outside is brown and crispy.

5. For the tomato sauce, add chopped tomatoes, water, crushed garlic, and tomato paste in a small skillet or saucepan, and sauté until tomatoes are soft and the sauce well blended.

6. When the rice is done, spread it on a serving platter. Sprinkle the onion-spice mixture over the rice, and place the chicken on top. Pass the tomato sauce to spoon onto individual plates.

Sadu Weaving

Sadu weaving is an embroidery form hand woven by Bedouin people that uses geometrical shapes. You can create your own weaving project by using construction paper.

Materials Needed
Construction paper of different colors
Scissors
White glue

1. Fold a square of construction paper in half; then fold it again.

2. With the closed end of the fold facing you, make cuts about an inch apart. Leave an inch margin at the top of the cut. This will create slits.

3. Open the paper and set aside. This is the base for your weave.

4. Take other colors of construction paper and cut them in one-inch strips.

5. Take those strips and weave them through the slits of the first piece of paper.

6. When finished, glue the end of the strips to the first piece of paper.

2300–1000 BCE   Dilmun civilization flourishes.

300 BCE   Greeks establish a settlement on Failaka Island.

623 CE   The Arabs defeat the Persians at the battle of Zat Al-Salassel in Kazima area.

1672   The town of Kuwait is settled.

1752   Sabah I Bin Jaber becomes ruler of Kuwait.

1760   A wall is built around Kuwait city.

1899   Mubarak the Great signs alliance with Great Britain.

1914   Kuwait's first desalination plant is commissioned.

1922   The first public library in Kuwait is established.

1938   Oil is discovered in Kuwait's Burgan oilfield.

1942   The first bank in Kuwait opens.

1946   The first Kuwaiti crude oil shipment is exported.

1950   Sheikh Ahmad Al-Jaber Al Sabah dies.

1957   The Social Affairs Department conducts the first population census.

1961   Kuwait and Great Britain's 1899 agreement is terminated.

1963   Kuwait becomes a member of the United Nations on May 14.

1980   Kuwait supports Iraq in the Iran-Iraq War.

1990   Kuwait is invaded by Iraq, prompting the first Gulf War.

2006   Sheikh Jaber dies. Sabah al-Ahmad is sworn in as new emir.

2008   Radical Islamists win more than half of the Parliament's fifty seats.

2009   Women gain the right to obtain passports without the consent of their husbands.

2010   Global oil prices rise, bringing a 20 percent increase in Kuwait's revenue.

2011   Perfume ad featuring Rihanna is censored to reveal less of the singer's skin. Amid mass upheavals in the Middle East to overthrow many Arab governments, Kuwaitis protest not to overthrow the emir, but rather to replace his prime minister.

Introduction

1. The Carolina Center for the Study of the Middle East and Muslim Civilizations, "Where Is the Middle East?" Alfred T. Mahan, 1902, http://www.unc.edu/mideast/where/mahan-1902.shtml
2. Ibid., Valentine Chirol, 1903, http://www.unc.edu/mideast/where/chirol-1903.shtml

Chapter One. Welcome to Kuwait!

1. History of Ikaria, http://www.island-ikaria.com/culture/history.asp
2. Jenny Walker, Stuart Butler, Terry Carter, Lara Dunston, and Frances Linzee Gordon, *Oman, UAE & Arabian Peninsula* (Oakland, CA: Lonely Planet, 2007).
3. CIA *World Factbook*, Kuwait https://www.cia.gov/library/publications/the-world-factbook/geos/ku.html
4. Ibid.
5. Ibid.

Chapter Two. Brief History

1. The Rich History of Kuwait, "From Flint Tools to Petrochemicals," 1Website Creative PTE, http://www.1website.com/c_t1_index/c_t1_index.html
2. Minnesota State University, "Ubaid," http://www.mnsu.edu/emuseum/cultural/oldworld/middle_east/ubaid.html
3. Frederick F. Anscombe, *The Ottoman Gulf: The Creation of Kuwait, Saudi Arabia, and Qatar* (New York: Columbia University Press, 1997).
4. Kuwaiti-Slovak Archaeological Mission, http://www.kuwaitarchaeology.org/
5. Michael Rice, *The Power of the Bull*, London: Psychology Press, 1998.
6. Official Web Site for the State of Kuwait, http://www.da.gov.kw/eng/picsandevents/riseofkuwait.php
7. General Consulate of the State of Kuwait, Los Angeles, http://www.kuwaitconsulate.org/About_Kuwait/About_Kuwait.html
8. Ibid.
9. United States Department of State, Kuwait, http://www.state.gov/r/pa/ei/bgn/35876.htm
10. Nicolè A. Staab, "Paradise Prevails," *Egypt Today,* http://www.egypttoday.com/article.aspx?ArticleID=7425

Chapter Three. Politics and Government

1. *The Estimate*, "Kuwait's Political System," June 4, 1999, http://www.theestimate.com/public/060499.html
2. United States Department of State, Kuwait, http://www.state.gov/r/pa/ei/bgn/35876.htm
3. Ibid.
4. *The Estimate.*
5. OM International, Country Profile: Kuwait, http://www.om.org/de/country-profile/kuwait
6. Embassy of the State of Kuwait, Stockholm, Sweden: "National Flag," http://www.kuwaitembassy.se/index.php?option=com_content&view=article&id=49&Itemid=56

Chapter Four. The Land

1. Kuwaiti-Slovak Archaeological Mission, http://www.kuwaitarchaeology.org/
2. Kuwait Info: Geography: Kuwait Islands, http://www.kuwait-info.com/a_state_of_kuwait/state_kuwait_gislands2.asp
3. Arabian Wildlife: "Kuwait," http://arabianwildlife.uaeinteract.com/archive/vol2.2/kuw.htm

Chapter Five. The Kuwaiti People

1. United States Department of State, Kuwait, http://www.state.gov/r/pa/ei/bgn/35876.htm
2. PBS, "Pilgrimage to Karbala; Sunni and Shia: The Worlds of Islam," *Wide Angle*, March 26, 2007, http://www.pbs.org/wnet/wideangle/episodes/pilgrimage-to-karbala/sunni-and-shia-the-worlds-of-islam/1737/

3. Ibid.
4. United States Department of State, Kuwait.
5. B. R. Mitchell, *International Historical Statistics: Africa, Asia & Oceania 1750-2000*, (Basingstoke: Palgrave MacMillan, 2003).
6. Dilip K. Das and Michael Palmiotto, *World Police Encyclopedia*: A-K, index (New York: Taylor and Francis, 2006).
7. United States Department of State, Kuwait.

Chapter Six. Kuwaiti Culture
1. *World Travel Guide*, "Kuwait City Nightlife," http://www.worldtravelguide.net/kuwait-city/nightlife
2. Maria O'Shea, and Michael Spilling, *Kuwait* (Tarrytown, NY: Marshall Cavendish, 2009), p. 127.
3. Ibid.
4. Bill Badley, "Sounds of the Arabian Peninsula 2000." In Simon Broughton and Mark Ellingham, with James McConnachie, and Orla Duane, (Ed.), *World Music, Vol. 1: Africa, Europe and the Middle East*, pp. 351–354. Rough Guides Ltd (New York, Penguin Books, 2000).

Chapter Seven. From Pearls to Pipelines
1. Embassy of the State of Kuwait, Stockholm, Sweden: History, http://www.kuwaitembassy.se/index.php?option=com_content&view=article&id=46:history&catid=34:kuwait&Itemid=27
2. Kuwait Petroleum Corporation, *Kuwait Oil History,* http://www.kpc.com.kw/AboutKPC/KuwaitOilHistory/default.aspx

3. Ibid.
4. "Best Countries for Business," *Forbes.com*, http://www.forbes.com/lists/2010/6/best-countries-10_Kuwait_CHI050.html
5. United States Department of State, Kuwait, http://www.state.gov/r/pa/ei/bgn/35876.htm
6. Ibid.
7. Ibid.

Chapter Eight. Famous Kuwaitis
1. "Born to Summit," *Everest News*, January 10, 2005, http://www.everestnews.com/stories004sec4002/zeddyeverest2004summits7.htm
2. Ibid.
3. *Trip Atlas*: Ahmad Meshari Al-Adwani. http://tripatlas.com/Ahmad_Meshari_Al-Adwani
4. Omar Hasan, "First Kuwaiti Woman Minister Breaks Mental Barrier," *Middle East Online*, March 8, 2006, http://www.middle-east-online.com/english/?id=15942
5. "Person of the Week: Dr. Massouma al-Mubarak," *ABC News*, January 17, 2005, http://abcnews.go.com/WNT/PersonOfWeek/story?id=859044&page=2
6. *SiloBreaker*, Biography for Massouma Al Mubarak, http://www.silobreaker.com/biography-for-massouma-al-mubarak-5_2260299693214924800_4
7. "Person of the Week: Dr. Massouma al-Mubarak."

Books

O'Shea, Maria, and Michael Spilling. *Kuwait*. Tarrytown, NY: Marshall Cavendish, 2009.

Rice, Earl, Jr. *Overview of the Persian Gulf War, 1990*. Newark, DE: Mitchell Lane Publishers, 2009.

Works Consulted

Anscombe, Frederick F. *The Ottoman Gulf: The Creation of Kuwait, Saudi Arabia, and Qatar*. New York: Columbia University Press, 1997.

Arabian Wildlife: "Kuwait."
http://arabianwildlife.uaeinteract.com/archive/vol2.2/kuw.htm

Badley, Bill. "Sounds of the Arabian Peninsula 2000." In Simon Broughton and Mark Ellingham, with James McConnachie, and Orla Duane (Ed.). *World Music, Vol. 1: Africa, Europe and the Middle East*. Rough Guides Ltd, New York: Penguin Books, 2000.

The Carolina Center for the Study of the Middle East and Muslim Civilizations.
http://mideast.unc.edu/

CIA *World Factbook*, Kuwait.
https://www.cia.gov/library/publications/the-world-factbook/geos/ku.html

Das, Dilip K., and Michael Palmiotto. *World Police Encyclopedia: A-K, index*. New York: Taylor and Francis, 2006.

The Estimate. "Kuwait's Political System." June 4, 1999.
http://www.theestimate.com/public/060499.html

Everest News. "Born to Summit." January 10, 2005.
http://www.everestnews.com/stories004sec4002/zeddyeverest2004summits7.htm

General Consulate of the State of Kuwait, Los Angeles.
http://www.kuwaitconsulate.org/About_Kuwait/About_Kuwait.html

Hasan, Omar. "First Kuwaiti Woman Minister Breaks Mental Barrier." *Middle East Online*, March 8, 2006.
http://www.middle-east-online.com/english/?id=15942

Kuwait Info
http://www.kuwait-info.com/

Kuwaiti Recipes
http://www.healthy-life.narod.ru/wor_ek113.htm

Kuwaiti-Slovak Archaeological Mission
http://www.kuwaitarchaeology.org/

Minnesota State University. "Ubaid."
http://www.mnsu.edu/emuseum/cultural/oldworld/middle_east/ubaid.html

Mitchell, B. R. *International Historical Statistics: Africa, Asia & Oceania 1750–2000*. Basingstoke: Palgrave MacMillan, 2003.

OM International, Country Profile: Kuwait.
http://www.om.org/de/country-profile/kuwait

PBS. "Pilgrimage to Karbala; Sunni and Shia: The Worlds of Islam." *Wide Angle*, March 26, 2007.
http://www.pbs.org/wnet/wideangle/episodes/pilgrimage-to-karbala/sunni-and-shia-the-worlds-of-islam/1737/

Person of the Week: Dr. Massouma al-Mubarak. *ABC News*. January 17, 2005.
http://abcnews.go.com/WNT/PersonOfWeek/story?id=859044&page=2

Rice, Michael. *The Power of the Bull*. London: Psychology Press, 1998.

The Rich History of Kuwait. "From Flint Tools to Petrochemicals." 1Website Creative PTE. http://www.1website.com/c_t1_index/c_t1_index.html

Walker, Jenny, Stuart Butler, Terry Carter, Lara Dunston, and Frances Linzee Gordon. *Oman, UAE & Arabian Peninsula*. Oakland, CA: Lonely Planet, 2007.

World Travel Guide. "Kuwait City Nightlife."
http://www.worldtravelguide.net/kuwait-city/nightlife

On the Internet
Countries and Their Cultures
http://www.everyculture.com/Ja-Ma/Kuwait.html

Culture Crossing, Kuwait
http://www.culturecrossing.net/basics_business_student.php?id=111

Culture of Kuwait
http://www.kuwaitiah.net/culture.html

Kuwait
http://iml.jou.ufl.edu/projects/spring06/eisa/culture.htm

PHOTO CREDITS: pp. 3, 28—Steve and Jemma Copley; pp. 10–11—Deep Gosh; pp. 18, 21, 32, 34—Ra'ed Qutena; p. 22—Department of Defense; p. 36—Neil Smith; p. 38—Keith Pomakis; pp. 46, 49—Cajetan Barreto. All other images—cc-by-sa-2.0. Every effort has been made to locate all copyright holders of material used in this book. If any errors or omissions have occurred, corrections will be made in future editions of the book.

aquifer (AK-wih-fur)—An underground, water-bearing rock.

Arab (AYR-ub)—A member of a Semitic people inhabiting much of the Middle East and North Africa.

emir (ee-MEER)—Commander or leader.

Fertile Crescent (FUR-tul KRES-ent)—The area of land arching from the Persian Gulf over the watersheds of the Tigris and Euphrates rivers in Iraq through the western coast of the Mediterranean into Egypt.

ghutra (GOO-trah)—Traditional Arabian cloth headdress.

hajj (HAHJ)—The pilgrimage to Mecca.

hajji (HAH-jee)—Arabic word for "pilgrim"; someone who makes the hajj.

insular (IN-suh-lur)—Isolated; having a narrow viewpoint.

jihad (jee-HOD)—Holy war.

Levant (leh-VONT)—The land area between Mesopotamia and Egypt.

millennium (muh-LEH-nee-um)—A period of one thousand years.

OPEC (OH-pek): Organization of Petroleum Exporting Countries. An organization comprised of major oil producing countries.

Palestinian (pal-uh-STIH-nee-un)—Of or relating to the area of Palestine and its inhabitants; Palestine is a historical term for the area that is now (approximately) Israel and the West Bank.

parliamentary (par-luh-MEN-tuh-ree)—Relating to a Parliament, the type of legislature used in Great Britain and certain other countries.

per capita (PUR KAP-ih-tuh)—For each individual; per person.

pilgrimage (PIL-gruh-midj)—A journey to a sacred place.

sheikh (SHEEK)—Leader of an Arab tribe or village.

souk (SOOK)—An Arabian marketplace.

tournette (TUR-net)—A revolving platter that is turned by hand and used to make pottery and to paint uniform bands around the pots.

Kathleen Tracy has been a journalist for over twenty years. Her writing has been featured in magazines including *The Toronto Star*'s "Star Week," *A&E Biography* magazine, *KidScreen*, and *TV Times*. She is also the author of numerous books for Mitchell Lane Publishers, including *We Visit Cuba; We Visit Saudi Arabia; The Fall of the Berlin Wall; Paul Cézanne; The Story of September 11, 2001; The Clinton View; Mariah Carey;* and *Kelly Clarkson*. Tracy lives in the Los Angeles area with her two dogs and African Grey parrot.